GARDENING

Other titles by Danny :-

Danny Gets to Grips with **Golf**
Danny Gets to Grips with the **Motor Car**
Danny Gets to Grips with **Horse & Pony Care**

Danny
GETS TO GRIPS WITH
GARDENING

DC Publishing Paperback

First Edition
Published in Great Britain 1995
by DC Publishing
11 Bryanston Village
Blandford Forum
Dorset DT11 0PR

Made and printed in Great Britain

For John,
my Father-in-law
(page 45),

who battles with the elements to spend every
day in his magnificent garden. Without fail,
each visit includes a guided tour. A spare set
of batteries is always at hand for a
torchlight inspection.

CONTENTS

FOREWORD

" No-one gardens for very long, especially in our climate, without realising that a sense of humour is an essential attribute.

The ability to smile through adversity is a characteristic of the true gardener and yet, strangely, very few artists and writers have been able to tap into this and produce works with a gardening theme that are truly amusing.

Certainly, good gardening cartoons have been as scarce as rocking horse manure; until now.

I have been greatly entertained by Danny's drawings and by his accurate perception of what makes gardening and gardeners tick; I'm sure you will be too."

Professor Stefan Buczacki

It's a good idea to consult with others in the
family so that you know just what they want!

First...Draw up a full and detailed plan.

Plot the shape of your potential garden,
remembering to view it from all angles.

Be nosey! Look at gardens in your area
and note down which plants do well.

Frequent watering will assist growth,
but patience is required.

Use mature trees as the backbone
of your planting scheme.

LAND CLEARANCE

Some aspects of gardening can be
combined with other leisure activities.

The Wheelbarrow
Ideal for the removal of all those
useless weeds.

Woody stems can be burnt,
but be sure that they are dry first.

Don't overdo it, a little slog every day or so
is better than one back-breaking blitz....

SOIL

You will soon realise if the the drainage
is poor... pools of water will appear
on the soil surface.

To disperse the water,
spike the area deeply.

Clay soil can be advantageous.

Sandy soil can be disappointing.

Chalky soil can be a worry.

Stoney soil can improve aeration.

Acidic soil can in certain circumstances
be mildly toxic.

If there is a hard impervious layer below
the topsoil causing poor drainage,
it must be broken up to let the water through.

No matter what your soil type, seek out the infamous
New Zealand earthworms and send them packing.

COMPOST

First, line the base of your compost
with surplus and waste paper....

and start it off with anything
organic.

Within a few weeks, your compost heap
will have grown significantly.

WATERING

The battle against water shortage begins
well before the dry days of summer.

During periods of water restriction,
domestic waste water from baths
will be perfectly usable in the garden.

For watering lawns, try to avoid the
open ended hose-pipe.....
Sprinklers are best!

A great invention and a must for all
gardeners is the new super jet spray gun,
but be sure the jet is adjusted to suit the use.

If you invest in a hosepipe, always coil it up
and store it out of full sunlight.

THE TOOL SHED

Before rushing out to buy brand spanking new tools,
there are a couple of other options.

Visit an elderly member of the family
whose gardening days may be numbered...
Should the relative decide that he and his tools
cannot be parted.....

Cast your eye in secondhand shops. Local
auction sales are great, but be careful not to
get too carried away.

If all attempts to find secondhand tools fail, visit your local gardening superstore, but beware of being bamboozled into buying tools you don't need.

Forget the macho image...choose tools
which are more comfortable to use.

DIGGING

There are 3 main methods of digging...

Single Digging

Double Digging & thirdly that
of which I am a great supporter...

Minor mechanical assistance digging.

TREES & SHRUBS

Tree surgery is the name given to
a form of pruning.

Take care when pruning or you may
be introduced to another form of surgery!

For hedge cutting shears can be used.

If you can afford it,
an electric trimmer is quicker.

The wheelbarrow is very useful for collecting hedge clippings etc., but be sure the load is well-balanced.

Ensure gates are wide enough for
wheelbarrow access.

Before buying shrubs at your local nursery,
check that the roots have not outgrown
the container.

It may be tempting to go for the larger specimens.

Small younger plants often have more chance of survival.

Even well tended favourites may die, be philosophical.

Half-hardy bedding plants are often killed
during frost periods, if left unprotected out of doors.

For privacy, one good idea is to plant an evergreen hedge.

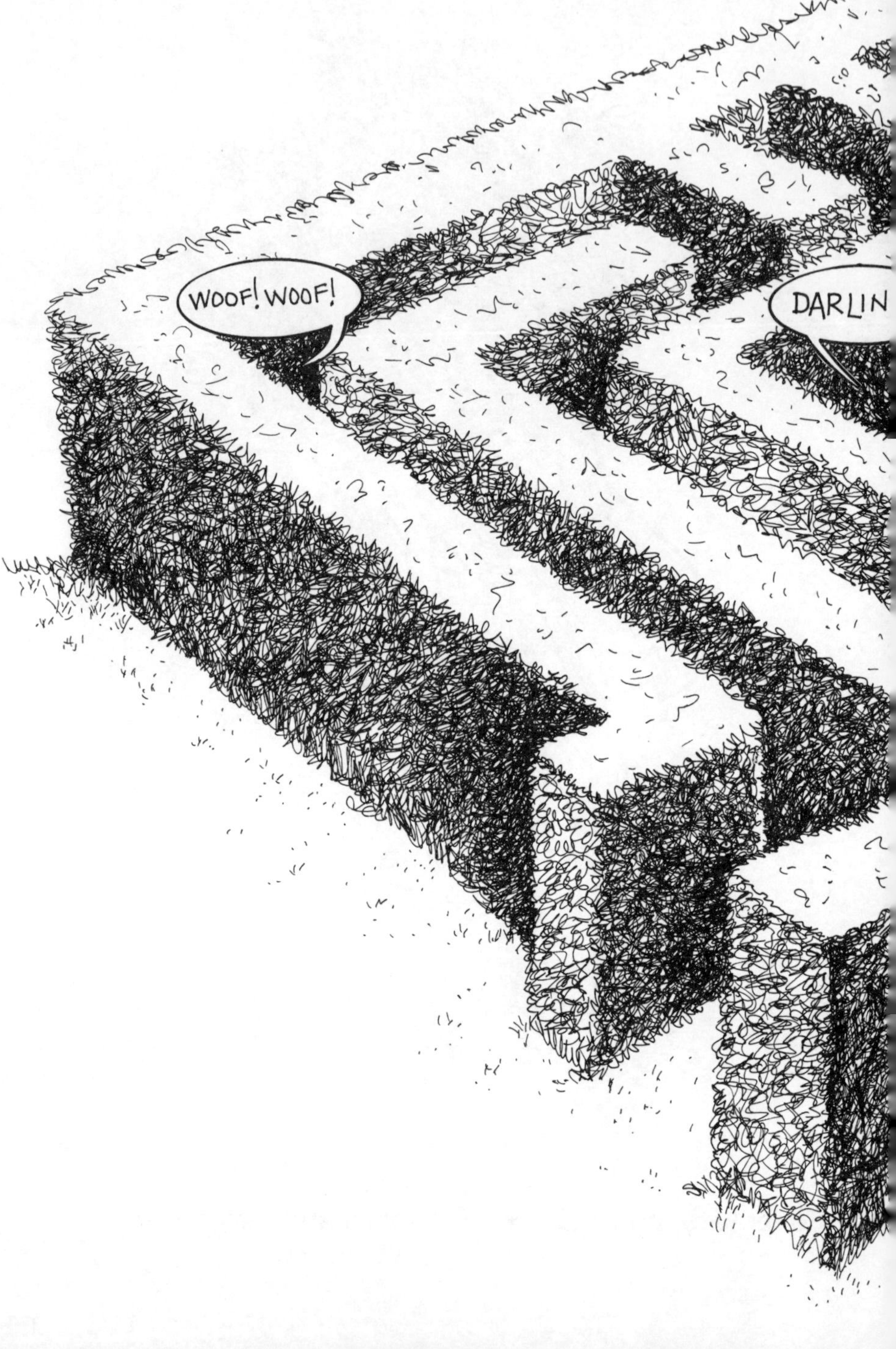
WOOF! WOOF!
DARLIN

For the reclusive character, build your own arbour.

THE ROCK GARDEN

Whether you build your rock garden modestly.....

....or rather ambitiously......

You'll have great fun in the making of it.
The best place is on a slight slope.

I said, "Slight slope!"

Once the rock garden has been built, now
is the time to collect your plants.

The sink garden is very popular
but siting should be given due thought.

Hang baskets to allow ease of access for visitors.

WATER GARDEN

Correct siting of your pond is of paramount importance.

Listen to unbiased advice if re-siting is required.

Think big and bold when building a water feature.

Make your pond simple in appearance....

Don't dig your pond too deeply as
planting may be difficult.

The range of plants and insects appearing
in your pond may surprise you.

Goldfish can provide many hours of pleasure.

THE LAWN

If you are faced with the task of
making a new lawn, share the work
with members of the family.

Make the site level....crouching down and
running your eye over the ground helps
you to spot any bumps and hollows.

It's a good idea to leave the site idle
for 3 or 4 weeks so that any
overlooked weeds can be removed smartly.

If you decide on turf, be sure to order the correct amount. Over-ordering can be wasteful and costly

If you decide to seed a lawn, order more than
the recommended quantity....
Birds are known to favour a nibble?

WEEDS

Weeds have a nasty habit of appearing from nowhere

The best and oldest method is to remove the
weeds by hand with roots intact.

If you think you're losing the war,
you may be provoked into using
more extreme measures....

WEED KILLER!

If all else fails, revert to plan B!